TERRIFIC *Kids*

TERRIFIC

Practical Principles

for Raising Kids with a

Strong Moral Compass

Gioconda A. Marroquín Suárez, BS, MDiv

TERRIFIC KIDS
Copyright © 2019 by Gioconda A. Marroquín Suárez, BS, MDiv

Printed in Canada

ISBN: 978-1-4866-1785-2

Word Alive Press
119 De Baets Street, Winnipeg, MB R2J 3R9
www.wordalivepress.ca

Cataloguing in Publication may be obtained through Library and Archives Canada.

Contents

Foreword   vii

A Word on Faith   ix

Introduction   xiii

The Arrival   1

     Discovery   2

     Teaching Respect   6

     Rules   8

     Correction   10

     Demands   13

     Outings   14

     Responsibility   15

     Challenges in Different Types of Families   17

     Learning from Your Children   18

     Communication   20

     Childhood Wounds   22

     Relationships   23

     Knowing Your Child   24

     Anger   25

     Teaching Values   28

     Grandparents   31

     Eating   33

Sleeping   34

Travelling   35

Eating Out   36

Shopping   38

Chores   39

Money   41

Pets   42

Homework   44

Hygiene   47

Conclusion   51

Acknowledgements   53

Foreword

Over the time we worked together as fellow counsellors, I came to hear Gioconda's parenting philosophy in clear, confident, and consistent terms. When I actually met her delightful children — Naty, Danny, Misa, Rafa and Annabella — I saw living proof that her methods bear fruit. Their parents instill qualities in them in what might seem effortless ways but in truth are planned and purposeful. These fortunate children are happy and kind, are joyfully engaged in athletic, artistic, musical and culinary pursuits, and most strikingly are individuals with independent ideas and points of view that they fearlessly but politely share with visiting adults such as me. They enjoy and are respectful of one another, they help and cooperate without prodding, they freely relate stories and personal experiences as well as hopes and plans. Best of all, they smile a lot. They are a treat to hang out with.

Undoubtedly personalities develop in large part due to genetic contributions. But what cannot be underestimated in this process is the committed work of parents who are determined that their children will grow up to be "good people." Gioconda and her husband deserve kudos for doing their part. I know readers will find her ideas not only practical and helpful but inspiring.

—Jeanette Pieczonka, MSW

A Word on Faith

Faith and spirituality have played an important role in my life and family. I believe that if I am going to teach my children about right and wrong, morality, values, and ethics, I need to have a worldview that serves as a source for these ideas. My intention in this section is to encourage parents to think about this basis for parenting. If this does not make sense to you, you can skip this section altogether. However, I imagine there may be readers who will be interested in this aspect of life. To you, I want to say that I believe wholeheartedly in the importance of teaching my children the concept of a transcendent God who has made moral laws, as well as natural laws that we need to keep in order to live in harmony with each other and with the natural world.

If God exists (I will refer to God as Him), He has revealed Himself to humanity as a benevolent guide, so we are not left wondering what ought to be and ought not to be. We all know that we must follow the laws of the land; if we don't abide by these laws, we will be duly notified of our violation and may end up paying for it. Laws serve the purpose of functionality, structure, and order. In the same way, God has given us an intellect that helps us differentiate between right and wrong. He has given us a conscience which arouses in us regret or guilt whenever we wrong someone. He also instills in us our parental instinct and desire to care for and sacrifice for our children.

The picture of a mother or father with their newborn is a most beautiful picture to see. To me, this is the picture God uses to inspire me to know Him as a father in an intimate way. God wants me to know that He loves me and cares for me, as I do my children.

Why is teaching about faith in God important to me in bringing up my children? First, it makes me aware that I am responsible to God for the lives of my children. I believe that one day I will be held accountable for how I have treated my children, how I trained them, the time I invested in them, the care, love, support, forgiveness, and tolerance I showed toward them. All of these are reflections of how God deals with us as His children.

Second, my children don't belong to me; they belong to God and will be responsible for themselves. God has put them in my care for such a short period of time. I need to take advantage of this time to instill in them respect, love, tolerance, justice, forgiveness, and mercy towards others. When I discipline or correct my children with the future in mind, I am looking at the desired result: mature and responsible adults with a good character of their own. I am not looking to create images of myself or to reproduce myself in them, but to help them discover and acknowledge their own personal selves, to strengthen their gifts, to understand their limitations, and to correct their egotism.

Finally, the time will come when my children, as they grow, will have to decide for themselves to take on the faith I have taught them, or to follow other paths. For now, I will provide them with an environment for knowing God, having faith, and understanding God's revelation as objective truth. I turn my desire into a prayer for them that they might continue the journey that God has prepared for them, even if the journey they decide on does not acknowledge Him. God has given us free will to seek Him or seek other things. In the end, we each must decide.

If faith in God is or becomes part of your home environment, make sure your teaching comes with openness for your children to dialogue, question, and explore alternatives as they grow up.

Introduction

You may be wondering about me: who is she? Where does she get her information? What sources does she draw on to back up the advice offered in this book?

I bring to the table my background as a family counsellor and teacher of adults, teens, and children. I have volunteered hundreds of hours at my children's public elementary school, observing teachers interacting with their classes, and learning how to help kids pay attention, follow direction and maintain a consistent structured routine. Above all I bring many years of dealing with the demands and joys of raising my own five kids. I bring a rich trove of personal observations, experiences, trials, and results in my life with my children. I don't consider myself an expert but if my insights here help a reader in some way, my goal will be met. I ask the reader to try to consider and recognize the principles that can be best applied in his or her own situation.

There are different philosophies of parenting. The approach I have used with my children is one that values structure, order, discipline, love, and morality, rather than following the lead of the child. I believe that parents are to be the authority in the home, not the children. Parents are the ones who provide a foundation of good leadership under the umbrella of a caring home. The Word of God has been key in providing the wisdom and producing the grace and patience needed in my parenting.

It is gratifying when people I don't know approach me and comment on the respectful behaviour of my children. I have received compliments about my well-behaved children from people at hotel resorts, on buses, on airplanes (people who tend to look anguished when they initially see my kids sitting close to them), as well as teachers and other parents. Sometimes they add, "Keep doing what you are doing because it works." It feels like a nice, reinforcing pat on the back.

In this book, I want to share some practical principles with adults (parents, caregivers, grandparents, aunts, uncles, babysitters, etc.) who may feel helpless when the children in their lives display unruly behaviour or disobedience. There are countless parenting books available, each offering tips or step-by-step guides for dealing with difficult behaviour. Often we don't know where to begin when searching for solutions. I hope to offer empathy and encouragement for this sometimes-tiring task we call parenting. I want to offer assurance that patience and persistence pay off.

I hope to inspire you, to motivate you, to make you laugh, to give you an opportunity to see that parenting is not an end but a means towards a goal: developing mature and responsible adults with a good character of their own. I want to encourage you to consider parenting with our children's future in mind because we have it in our power to shape the kinds of citizens our society needs.

The examples I use are real scenarios, although I have changed some circumstances to avoid breaking any confidentiality and trust with the people I've had the opportunity to observe.

Special thanks to all the people who have had any type of influence in my life, and especially to my kids for allowing me to always examine my parenting skills, grow as a person, and become a better parent. It is with them in mind that I was pushed to scribble these thoughts on paper.

The
Arrival

Babies are a blessing to every family, a blessing that comes with the responsibility to nurture them into their own selves. They each come with their own temperament, personality, abilities, and strengths.

Bringing a newborn home is a time of transition for parents and/or caregivers, one that includes excitement, fear, and anxiety. While a baby does not arrive with a companion guide on "how to handle me," a firstborn child teaches us how to parent.

Sometimes we feel fear and anxiety in not knowing how to handle the demands that come with our new baby. Our baby will not respect our schedule, times for rest or meals. In some cases, nights seem to be the times that our newborn chooses to be most awake, most hungry, or most gassy. Night can be when our baby experiences discomfort and needs many changes of diapers and clothing. All of these seem to happen when the parent is exhausted, when we feel like we will lose our mind.

We may think, "I didn't sign up for this" and may begin to doubt our sense of being a fit parent. We may become more sensitive to the opinions of other people such as extended family members, close friends, neighbours, doctors or nurses, perceiving their opinions or innocent comments as criticism of our parenting skills.

At the same time, of course, other family members can relieve new-parent anxiety by helping and giving us a break from the demands of the newborn. Parents who do not have the extended support of family members may need to look to the community for support. Some community churches, for example, run support programs for parents by allowing them to participate in a "coffee break" that provides child care. There are parent-and-tots programs run at community centres where both parent and infant can be involved. Parents can ask their family doctor or nurse for activities and programs being offered. Many parents even find walking around a mall with an infant in a stroller to be a good way to get out of the house, meet other parents and get involved in what the community is offering. The more we seek support, entertainment, and education, outside of our daily routine, the better we will be able to handle stress that comes with caring for a newborn.

Discovery

Apart from the obvious tasks of feeding and changing our newborn, our first job upon the arrival of our baby is to discover who this new person is. Parents need to teach their infant how to build trust in a secure environment. The baby has come from the most secure and nurturing place—the womb—to a noisy and yet unknown world. The newborn knows no limits, no rules, and no boundaries.

To help the new baby to experience a healthy attachment to their primary caregiver (who could be mother or father or someone else), I suggest parents establish a schedule consisting of feeding times, talking, playing, reading, holding, and just being together.

At the beginning, for the first few days or weeks, the baby will set the rhythm of what, when, and how things are done. When we begin to take charge of the schedule, we can plan for time for ourselves where we can recharge and rest, eat without rushing or interruption, take a bath, read a book, or socialize with other adults. If we make time to self-nurture, then we will be recharged and more available to care for our newborn.

The schedule, established as a routine, will help teach the newborn that decisions are made by the parent who is responsible for his or her care. The baby will sound an alert by fussing or crying. The parent learns the difference between cries of discomfort, pain and attention. By having a consistent schedule, the baby will learn that he is loved and cared for.

Consistency will establish the child's attachment to and healthy dependency on their parent. This is very important, because a healthy sense of attachment leads to trust that will later help the child develop healthy independence, emotional maturity, and connection to other significant adults. A planned schedule also results in a child's ability to self-regulate and function independently.

For instance, when each of my five children were very small, I included play time with my infant in our schedule. I made sure to take time to interact through such play, whether it was sitting on the floor, singing, playing peekaboo, kissing, or just enjoying each other. After the play time, I would leave the infant alone, but not out of sight, and take time to do other things around the house that needed to get done. At first, when I did my other tasks, my baby would cry and demand my attention. However, I felt that if the baby was fed, clean, not sick and had received one-on-one time with a parent, it was safe to let him or her be alone with appropriate supervision. Learning how to comfort and settle oneself down is a life skill that teaches children to handle discomfort.

Infants come into the world with an instinct to survey, explore, and discover their surroundings. As they grow, they will want to get their hands into anything they think is appealing or that attracts, without knowing the dangers they might encounter. This might be getting close to the stove, putting fingers in electrical outlets or any other hazard. Should the parent baby-proof their house? I did not as I believed that this stage was a great time to teach my newly mobile children about limits and boundaries.

But parents know their own children best. If you feel that it is best to put a gate over a doorway to prevent your toddler from falling down the stairs, go ahead and do so. (Also, parents dealing with children with health issues require an altogether different and unique set of guidelines.) But as you are putting up the gate, my advice is to make it a teachable moment, explaining that the gate is there for their safety. As the child grows, the parent can explain that in life there are limits that need to be respected; this can be a place to explain to children that they can voice their own limits and that these need to be respected, but that they also need to respect other people's limits. Taking down a gate can be a time of celebration of a child's increased maturity and understanding of limits.

My goal was that a simple "no" would be a strong enough word to use in setting limits for my children. When it is, there is no need for explanation. I have found that the more parents try to explain their reasoning to the child, the more frustrated they become and the more opportunity (and power) is given to the child to question and protest against the parents' limits. Once a child learns to accept and not challenge a parent's authority, limits can be explained, enabling the child to internalize their motivation for obedience. Praise and affirming words can serve as motivation or incentive so that the child realizes that it feels good to obey their parent.

At some point, parents will notice that their child uses the word "no" as part of his or her everyday vocabulary. Usually, during this phase (which can vary age-wise) children are trying to assert themselves and beginning to establish some of their own limits. This is an opportune time to teach children the importance of sharing and to not just say "no" every time some other child wants to grab their toys, for example. At the same time the child is liberally experimenting with the word "no," he or she can be encouraged to say "yes" to give permission to others to borrow possessions or to follow a parent's direction.

Rather than fighting a child's use of the word "no," I always have tried to direct it in ways where a "no" is acceptable. In this way, the words "no" and "yes" will be the child's tool for distinguishing between what is appropriate and what is not.

A scheduled routine is valuable in that it provides consistency and security to a child, and at the same time it allows the parent to have free time to use as she or he pleases. I have always found this brings rhythm and harmony to the lives of both parent and child. When I take time for myself, I try to use it wisely, prioritizing what is most important. I always find it useful to ask myself whether it is more important, for instance, to rest or to complete a household chore. Using the time wisely means asking myself, "What do I need?" and not "What do I need to do?" If a parent is at the point of exhaustion, the laundry can wait and taking care of oneself is paramount.

A child will not build a healthy emotional connection with an angry, disturbed, or resentful mother or father. Neither will that exhausted parent have energy or desire to spend time with his or her partner. I have seen that the couple relationship tends to suffer the most in such situations.

There are simple tests to help a parent realize that prioritizing needs to happen in his or her life: when she finds herself aware that her irritation has increased; when he never seems to have enough time for the completion of a task; when tiredness is her constant emotional state; when he does not even have time for self-care or private functions such as having a shower.

As the parent adjusts his or her parenting approach to make sure their own needs are met, children will learn to respect their parent's schedule, as well as the *fact* that their demands can wait. Through learning to delay gratification, the child will develop the character quality of patience. This is a lesson many adults have not learned. How many adults live miserably because they do not know how to respect other people's limits or others' timing? They have not learned the lesson that life is not about "getting my way." They have yet to discover that through love, respect and service to others one can contribute to a better world. This demands sacrifice and altruism while "getting my way" arises from an egocentric heart.

Teaching Respect

By laying this foundation, we teach principles, values, and the importance of respect so that children learn to respect limits, to be patient, and to prioritize needs.

A strong-willed child will put a fight, but a parent does not need to give in to the child's demands. I encourage parents to be persistent in their efforts to teach children who is in charge and how to respect authority. In the process, as parents, we build our children's character strengths for success in life.

While I strongly advocate for parents to be the authority in the home, I also firmly believe that parental teaching needs to be based on love, care, trust, consistency, and respect of one's child as an individual human. If a parent doesn't build a healthy connection with his or her child, their authority will be challenged, and they may be regarded as an uncaring task master. A parent constantly affirms their child as valued and unique. A positive spoken word can build up a life; negative words destroy it. In a positive, nurturing milieu, a child will grow to feel secure about who he or she is and will grow in confidence. Positive words together with smiles and genuine hugs, cuddles, and other loving touches will reinforce a child's sense that he or she is valued, appreciated, and loved. When the parent is not available, a child with a strong sense of attachment will not feel threatened or abandoned.

The principle of respect is taught by giving respect. Children learn respect and how to show it from their parents. The best way to teach children respect is to show them respect, and to model it through the way parents respect each other as well as how they refer to and or treat others. Disagreeing with others while still respecting them is a skill that can be modelled for young children; it is a skill that equips children for dealing with bullying behaviour and for preventing it in themselves.

Along with respect, children need to be given space where they learn to voice their opinions and feelings in a healthy way. We can tell our child that it is okay to be upset, but it is not acceptable to mistreat others because of anger. This is an important lesson even for adults, many of whom still think that feeling angry entitles them to be disrespectful or abusive towards others. Others have learned only to keep their difficult or contrary feelings and thoughts to themselves, often leading to emotions that become too much to bear, and anger that is then expressed inappropriately.

Rules

I look at rules as a parent's tools which are used in creating boundaries for the child's own protection, for the respect of other people's limits, and for the enjoyment of the parent-child relationship.

Providing rules for our children prepares them to have order, stability, organization and a sense of security in their life. Rules of conduct are what maintain a society, a school, a church, a community centre, or a workplace. They are what keep relationships thriving. In order to interact with others, there must be a sense of what I am responsible for and what other people's responsibilities are towards me.

A parent must exercise his or her authority for the well-being of the child and not for selfish or personal motives. The point of disciplining unruly behaviour, mischievous acts, lies or other forms of dishonesty is not that these things annoy us in the moment, but that people don't tolerate these behaviours in the wider world. Through discipline, the child learns that such behaviours will not be tolerated in his or her world either.

The task of discipline is arduous, challenging, and sometimes tiring for parents. I always remind myself that the goal of discipline is the future—when my children become responsible and caring adults—and that I should not let myself get stuck in present inconveniences and discomforts. When our children become responsible and caring adults, we experience satisfaction, knowing that they have learned life skills, respect for others, and resilience. As parents, we will be content to know that we were part of the formation of our children's character.

If we bring up a child in a way that says we expect that he or she must pay us back for all the sacrifices we have made on their behalf, we are perhaps unconsciously exercising authority with selfish or personal motives. No parent should say or even hint, "I have given you everything, so now you owe me" or "After all I have done for you, this is how you repay me?" There is nothing wrong with wanting our children to recognize the investment we have made in their lives and characters; the mistake lies in bringing up a child with this as expectation.

One of my purposes in raising my children is to invest in and cultivate a guilt-free, loving, gracious, and respectful relationship with them. As children mature, they need to understand that everything the parent does is in the children's best interest and is given according to the best of the parent's capacity at the time. The results that this will bring will be pleasant and positive as the grown child will desire a lasting relationship of mutual support and love with their parent.

By contrast, a parent who is permissive, has an attitude of indifference towards the children's behaviour, or uses discipline for his own purposes is running a school for tyrants. Children need boundaries and correction for the formation of a healthy character. The older children get, the more challenging correction becomes. It is easier to begin as early as possible, which is why I recommend that it begins by using a schedule with your baby.

I suggest parents make lists of rules for different situations including house rules, dinner-time rules, rules while in the car, and rules for visiting other people's homes. Rules should be given as the situation or demand arises. Every rule should have a goal in mind, such as teaching punctuality. It can be a mistake to think of rules as confining, restricting and inconvenient. Rather, they offer security and are freeing in that they allow for the development of personalities that succeed. (Parents should avoid sending mixed messages when expecting obedience from the child. If a rule changes because of an unforeseen circumstance and the child is older than five years of age, a simple explanation is sufficient. Changes to rules should be the exception and not the norm.)

Correction

Children learn by watching their parents' behaviour and imitating it. This can motivate us to model appropriate conduct for our children. By telling young children what they must do and not do, the child is socialized or educated to become a member of the society in which they will live.

As we know, however, children don't always behave appropriately. Every undesired action must be corrected by the parent. But the method of correction also matters as our young child looks to us for approval and validation of their behaviour.

Therefore, correction needs to be done with love as its motive and not anger. In the course of moulding an excellent character, a parent wants to nurture a healthy relationship with their child. Love here means that the parent wants what is best for their child and applies it, even if it hurts temporarily. In the long run, the result of good discipline is a mature character and not a person who feels entitled, angry or resentful.

I encourage parents to remember that correction must never be done in anger. This is when we make the most parental mistakes. An angry parent may humiliate his or her child (by screaming, name-calling or intimidating the child physically). A child who experiences this type of correction will internalize authority as negative and will have problems accepting and respecting authority. As parents, we need to learn how to present ourselves as a positive authority figure to our children, with respect guiding the relationship. In dealing with a testy situation, I remind myself to pause, calm myself down and then come back to deal with the behaviour. Taking time to breathe and think it through does not mean we are ignoring the problem. Dealing with the situation when we are calm and in control enables children to see that authority is there to aid them.

We also make mistakes when we are tired: a weary parent may be tempted to overlook a child's unwanted behaviour. It is better to correct in love than to avoid dealing with the matter.

Often parents spend a lot of time explaining to children ideas that their under-developed minds cannot yet understand. Short and simple commands work better than lengthy explanations with young children. It is better to give one rule or instruction at a time until the child learns to follow and trust the parent's judgment.

After children learn to follow instructions, it is important to compliment and affirm them. Many parents only give attention to their children when they misbehave, while good behaviour seldom gets noticed. In order to help children with their own self esteem, parents need to pay attention to all behaviour. When the child obeys, I suggest offering them attention and limited praise. (By limited praise I mean that showing approval for the child should not become the only reward for or reinforcer of good behaviour. We want to avoid a scenario where the child concludes "I will behave so that Mom or Dad will be pleased with me." Our goal is that the child acknowledges what is best for him or her, apart from parental praise.)

I always evaluated my child's attitude as part of correction. For example, if a child has a desire to cooperate with others—such as helping prepare a cookie recipe—but is clumsy in handling the ingredients and ends up messing up the kitchen, the parent might get frustrated at the mess and fail to see the child's desire to help. I try to keep in mind the fact that children are not as coordinated or experienced as adults, so I offer them simpler tasks before giving them more complex ones. Mixing dough is easier than measuring ingredients so I allow my child to feel successful by accomplishing the simpler task. What is most essential is that parents watch for their children's attitude and respond to it appropriately, perhaps saying, "That was a good try" or "You helped a lot."

Once as I was watching my eldest son playing with his younger sibling, I noticed he had an attitude that said, "I am in charge. You do as I say!" I was grateful that I saw my kids sharing and playing, but my eldest son's attitude got my attention. This became a moment to teach him by guiding him toward the proper attitude when playing with others. I told my elder son that just because he is playing with someone younger than him does not make him "the boss" of the situation. In general, I believe that children should be left to decide what and how to play. If they are not able to agree, my children know they can come to me so I can arbitrate between them, but I've let them know that they might not like my decision so they might prefer to settle it among themselves first.

I believe that, while it is vital for the parents to affirm their children by saying how much they are loved regardless of their actions, obedience to the parent is essential. The reward of this will be that others will enjoy the child's presence on account of their good behaviour and attitudes. Listen to feedback from people who spend time with our children, such as their teachers: they can report back on the attitude our children display toward others. Notice and celebrate when children offer compassion, generosity, care, service, respect, and altruism towards others.

If a child persists in misbehaving, I believe that we need to reflect on a proper way to get the child's attention. That reflection should take into account the individual child's temperament and personality along with different options to offer when correcting. Whatever works best in achieving the desired outcome is the one I encourage the parent to use, while whichever method does not work should not be repeated. Sometimes I've seen that we can make child-rearing more challenging by failing to recognize what is *not* working. We may try harder, scream louder, impose a consequence we will not be able to follow through, and then end up undervaluing the notion of discipline altogether by doubting and questioning our capabilities as parents, asking, "Why is it not working?"

When parents feel we are stuck in a dead-end situation or feel helpless, our human tendency is to ignore the unwanted behaviour, to continue to use the same approach without achieving the desired results, and to isolate ourselves from others out of fear of being criticized. This, of course, is a lose-lose scenario: our child is deprived of necessary guidance and we feel defeated. Instead, this is a good time to look for outside support and help.

Demands

Parents need to teach their kids how to ask properly, and how to wait. The parent may say, "You may have your snack right after you pick up your toys." Messages such as, "You may watch television when you stop crying and ask properly" will guide the child in the proper way to request what they want. If your child simply demands something, do not give it to him or her; rather, teach them the proper way to request things.

It is easier and better to mould the temperament of a child than that of an adult. It is better to hear threatening and manipulating phrases from a young child (such as "you don't love me," "you prefer…" or "I will not…") than to see your grown child lose a job or get a divorce because they never learned how to treat people respectfully. You can choose which discomfort is preferable, present or future.

Rules of conduct that are not tolerated in the real world should not be tolerated at home. Behaviours we don't like to see in others should not be accepted from our children.

Outings

We have all seen children cause a scene in a shopping centre in order to get their own way. This does not have to be the way, nor should parental authority be negotiated. When a child is obedient, life is fun, exciting and easy to enjoy. We are able to take our child anywhere.

In order to have this pleasant experience, we can adapt methods that work well for children when we prepare to take them on outings.

Depending on the age of my child, I always feed the child before the outing and let them know where we are going. If history showed that the child will likely want something out of the outing, I lay out rules about the outing in advance. Afterwards, when an outing has gone well according to my expectations, I might occasionally treat my child to a snack or a small reward at the end.

Whenever my family is invited to eat at other people's homes, I feed my kids beforehand so that our visit can be more about the people we are visiting and less about what or when we are eating. I have no control over the time of the actual meal that will be served or whether it will be food that we as a family are used to eating. Feeding my kids beforehand lessens the chance that my kids will make the host uncomfortable. I also don't have to worry that they will be hungry.

When visiting other people's home, my children know that they should follow the same rules that they follow at home: going off to play when they are dismissed from adult socializing; not playing with objects that are not toys; no screaming or fighting; asking permission to take things; saying please and thank you; and, putting things back in their place. Before leaving our house, I give short and simple rules of what is expected. After the outing, children need to hear feedback with affirmation or correction, whether about the good time we all had or how to have a better time. I also note the feedback from the host if they extend another invitation. This is a fantastic opportunity to teach children how to behave with others, and in other people's homes.

Responsibility

Teaching our children responsibility as early as possible will produce a child who takes initiative in caring for his or her own things and will save a parent from exhaustion. For instance, a child can learn to put everything back where it belongs. The parent can demonstrate the behaviour we expect of the child, and, using simple language, tell our child to do the same. After the child follows the instruction, we can offer a word of affirmation and praise. Toddlers want to mimic their parents and enjoy helping so this is a great opportunity for us to teach responsibility by encouraging the toddler in activities like helping us pick up clothes or putting clothes in the laundry basket.

Cultivating and nurturing this desire to be helpful sets the stage for the child to internalize behaviour that will become part of his or her nature. Through repetition and rewards, this forms valuable lifelong habits.

Chores are an important part of everyday family life. I will say more on this later but when anyone, parent or child, does chores, it is a way of telling others in the family, "I love you and I will take care of our shared home." By allowing your child the opportunity to do some routine chores, parents send the message, "You are an important part of this family and this family needs you as much as you need it." What better way to help build your child's self-esteem than by providing an opportunity to exercise responsibility as well as membership and belonging. The goal is not only helping your child feel needed and part of the family but ingraining in him or her the habit of responsible behaviour.

When children are older this sense of responsibility may extend to the timing of giving a child a cell phone, for instance. How will a parent know if their child is responsible enough to get a cell phone? Age is no indicator of responsibility. The parent can investigate by testing the child through giving him or her an object to care for. If the child is responsible for something small, then he or she can be responsible for something larger.

When it comes to providing children with the latest toys and gadgets, parents need to consider their own history. Parents who experienced deprivation in their childhood might feel guilty if they don't provide their children with the latest gadgets available in the market, not wanting their kids to miss out, especially when kids report that their friends have them. By contrast, a parent raised with a strong sense of thrift and belief that experiencing want builds strength might arbitrarily withhold useful and affordable things from their children. Be aware of how these factors influence you so that you can make conscious decisions. Above all, don't compare yourself with other parents and feel pressured to do the same with your kids. We need to use our own standards to evaluate what our own children would realistically benefit from.

No person can benefit if, instead of learning how to rely on himself or herself, he or she expects others to be responsible for him, pick up after him, and bail him out of trouble. The family provides a glimpse of what the real world is about. The family should be a place where children learn what responsibility is and where they are given life skills that equip them to answer the demands of society.

The family should be a place where values, morality and finding meaning in life are cultivated; it is where well-being is practised and mistakes are allowed and learned from. All such nurturing equips children to manage the demands of society. The family is the place where children learn about what is a priority and what is unimportant.

Challenges in Different Types of Families

Single parenting can be very challenging especially if you don't have extended family support. Such situations call for extra self-nurturing and outside help. Perhaps a friend can help with babysitting or favours can be exchanged with other parents in support of one another. Community groups such as single-parent groups can offer insights, experience, and a network of support and encouragement for the lone parent. It is comforting and reassuring for a single parent to know that they are not alone during this period of their life, that others struggle too.

In a home composed of two working parents, the challenge may be achieving consistency, especially if children know they take advantage of a parent's perceived weaknesses, such as tiredness and low tolerance for debates. Parents need to be united in the rules and consequences they give to their children. We need to take care to not allow the child to split us, to set parents against each other in matters of rules or discipline. I can think of times when one of my children wanted to watch a television show and asked one parent for permission. One parent would respond with, "No, not until you get your school work done" only to have the child go to the other parent to ask the same thing. If you do not check with the other parent, they may give permission without knowing that they have undermined your authority. Children learn to do this very early. However, if the child sees that both parents are constantly communicating with each other, this will rarely happen.

As parents, we also need time to be with each other, and children should not take all their parents' time. Parents should be able to sit and talk without being constantly interrupted by our children. We need time to relax after a day's work so we can more fully engage with and spend time with our children. If the parent gives all their time to the child without taking some time to breathe after work, the parent will, most likely, succumb to the demands of the child, parent out of guilt for not being there during the child's day, or will be irritable and frustrated when relating to their child.

Learning from Your Children

While we teach our children how to treat people in relationships, we can also learn from our children. I know that I have learned simplicity and openness from my children. If you take time to sit and watch your children at play, you will enter their world and you will be amazed at what you can learn. Let them teach you about themselves through the way they play and interact with their toys, objects, and other children. We are often caught up in an adult world and thus forget how to be simple and spontaneous, living life as it unfolds. We can enter our child's world and learn how to be a kid again and how this simplicity is needed in daily living.

Children also teach adults how to live in the present. Children fight, but a few minutes later they will continue to play together. A child will often forget what offended them and will not hold it against the other. Children teach us adults that many offenses are best forgotten, that ownership needs to be taken for mistakes, and that friendship can continue despite past conflicts.

Not only will the parent learn from his child, but the parent will enter the child's world, will learn about their child, and will be better able to relate to him or her. Children express their emotions through play. If the parent sees violent behaviour in the way their child plays, the parent should take the time to ask the child if he or she is frustrated or upset about something. A parent might be able to find out more about what is going on inside their child by playing with him than by talking or questioning him. Perhaps the child needs help that the parent can then figure out how to provide.

Some parents demand obedience, understanding and respect from their children, forgetting to build a relationship based around understanding the children's interests, attitudes, curiosities, and struggles. We teach children to obey and follow parental guidance not only because the parent is the authority but also so that children learn to trust and accept the guidance and wisdom that the parent offers. Spending time participating together in activities both parent and child enjoy can also provide a setting for communication.

Communication

I believe it is important for parents to allow children to be a part of family conversations where children feel free to express themselves and feel confident that others are listening.

This doesn't mean that there are no rules. Some rules about speaking can include: don't interrupt others when they are talking but wait for your turn; ask permission to speak; respect other opinions even when you don't agree with what you are hearing; and, always listen before talking. I've always told my children that we were given us two ears and one mouth for a reason—to do more listening than talking.

I've also always emphasized to my children not to judge others' feelings or make assumptions about what others might be feeling, but rather to evaluate observable behaviour. It's important to teach children the difference between communicating feelings through language such as "I feel" versus communicating thoughts through language such as "I think." If children can learn to understand these distinctions, they can become great communicators. For example, if my ten-year-old son feels left out by his peer group at school because they are not including him in their play, my son needs to learn to say, "I feel ignored and left out since you are not including me in the game," rather than, "You don't care about me." The former conveys my son's personal feelings while the latter is a judgment based on an assumption about the other person's intentions. Assumptions may be false and therefore need to be checked out with a clear message about how the other's behaviour makes you feel. This gives the other person a chance to say, "I wasn't aware. I am sorry." We need to teach our children how to check out what others mean if their behaviour is confusing or hurtful. In this way we are teaching them to avoid misconceptions and frustration.

It is important to get children involved in discussions around family decisions. Children will not make the decisions—this is the responsibility of the adult—but children can play an important part by contributing different perspectives, especially as they get older. I know of a family that was contemplating becoming foster parents. They sat their children down and expressed to them their desire to foster, wanting to know what their children thought about the idea. The parents had agreed between themselves that they would not begin a fostering initiative if their kids were against it since fostering requires an investment of energy on the part of every member of the family. In the end, the children were very excited by this idea and the family became a foster family.

There are other decisions about which parents may not need to consult their children. However, if parents have teens and the decision to go on vacation arises, for example, it makes sense for the parent to discuss vacation ideas not only because the teenager might have to negotiate time off from their part-time job, but also because teenagers are old enough to express preferences and take part in planning a family trip.

Children need to know and feel that they are important members of the family and that what they think will be considered. For parents with quiet children who have their own imaginary world or who feel more comfortable keeping their thoughts to themselves, one-on-one talks and trying to understand your child's way of thinking is important. We can help our children express their emotions or thinking by asking open-ended questions. I use questions such as, "What do you mean?" or I say, "Give me an example of what you mean. What would your perfect vacation look like?" Patience is needed whether our children are chatty or whether their words do not come out easily.

Childhood Wounds

Sometimes parents resist offering discipline to a child or are afraid of their own ability to care properly for their children as they may have internalized their own childhood wounds.

I have met people who have shared with me their stories of how they were neglected emotionally and physically by their parents, or how their parents were so busy that they felt lonely as they were growing up. Despite the comforts and treats that were available to them, they seldom remembered a time of connection or deep caring. Even as adults, these parents wonder why their own parents did not love them enough, or why they are still not interested in sharing in their present life.

We don't parent in a vacuum; we bring our backgrounds, our sense of who we are, into parenting. If an adult, now a parent, has not dealt with past wounds through forgiveness or healing, it is very likely that the parent will transmit the hurt to his or her own children. I encourage parents experiencing this to look for help in healing old wounds that could be affecting their parenting.

We need to be honest with ourselves, with our spouse and kids, and to own what we need to work on. There is empowerment when children hear from their parents that they are working on becoming better persons and thus better parents.

When we don't do this, sometimes our old wounds lead us to become completely absorbed in our child's life and end up giving to the child without limits. We may want to ensure our children receive what we ourselves were deprived of and so we go to the opposite extreme.

Deciding to stop the cycle of hurt is vital. Breaking the cycle of hurt and healing from past pain will help a parent acknowledge and accept the blessings that children are in our life. It will give children a healthy parent, one who is moderate and not anxious. In the end, both parent and children will reap the benefits. If you had an abusive or neglectful parent, then you yourself need to work towards acceptance of your history, making peace with your past, healing and learning to enjoy your current situation, and recognizing the treasures that are your children.

Relationships

Investing time in your kids and giving them the best of you is natural and expected. A problem, I believe, arises when the parent ceases to be herself or himself in the process. When this happens, we have neglected to care for our own needs. We become extremely sensitive to our child's needs, always on the alert for anything that might come up. Through this over-focus on the child, we can become distracted from the important requirement of cultivating and enriching our intimate relationship with our partner.

I know many mothers who first have a relationship with their children and, only if time allows, with their spouse. Children have become the centre of many couple relationships. The home is centred around the children. Decisions are made by the children. In many homes, we've moved far from the old saying that "Children should be seen and not heard" to a belief that says, in effect, that, "Children are not only seen but are dictating what is heard." We need to guard our relationship with our spouse for the sake of the children. If the couple partnership suffers, the children's sense of security will suffer. If this has happened in your relationship, I advise you to rescue yourself from this unhealthy way of relating. As your partner relationship is strengthened and grows more in unity and love, your children will have a solid foundation of healthy support.

Sometimes it is helpful to seek professional help, while at other times we can simply affirm ourselves as parents. A woman I knew kept questioning why her father didn't contact her even once a year. She felt neglected and wondered what she had done that had offended her father. She would call him but he would not return her phone calls. She asked to visit him; he said he was busy. For a long time, she had concluded that when her parents separated when she was a child must have been caused by something she did. Years later, now a mother of three, she had to face her past and learn to forgive, let go, and accept the limits her father has put on their relationship.

Knowing Your Child

As parents, we need to learn what our children's strengths and hidden gifts are in order to let go of a desire to mould our children in our own image. We need to nurture our children's own temperament. Sometimes parents' insecurities can lead to over-protection of our children; we don't want them to make their own mistakes, but to learn from ours. We try to protect them from the consequences of their choices, not realizing that children can learn about their own strengths (and weaknesses) through experiencing consequences. To be able to learn from their mistakes leads to the development of life skills that will be helpful to our children when they are encountering life challenges as they grow.

The more a parent tries to get involved and over-stresses about his or her parenting skills, the less likely he or she will see the desired changes in their children. As a child grows and becomes independent in his movements, words, choices, and decisions, parenting becomes more of a function of coaching the child. The more children mature, the less they should need the parent and the more the relationship becomes one of equality, trust, support, and respect.

Similarly, children need to have time alone to understand that it is fine to be alone, that there is no danger. Children need time with their parent and time away from the parent. She or he will learn how to trust that the parent will return and that he or she will not be abandoned. That is why we have daycare, friends, community support, and extended family to help in the upbringing of our children. Grandparents, aunts, uncles, and close family friends who invest in children's lives can provide them with an emotionally robust upbringing and also relieve some of the stresses parenting brings.

Anger

What to do when your child is angry? Anger needs to be understood as a natural and common emotion that we have for our own protection. Anger is a way of expressing and communicating a sense of personal violation or injury. It is important to explain to your child what anger is so he or she can accept it and learn how to express it in a healthy way. There is nothing wrong with feeling angry for a reason. Anger should be acknowledged and managed appropriately soon after an injury occurs.

I have tried to use common and metaphorical language to explain anger to my children. For example, anger is like an alarm system installed in your body. Whenever somebody hurts you in any way or you feel something wrong has been done to you, your alarm goes off and you experience an angry response.

As parents, we teach our children how to deal with anger through modelling and describing proper behaviour when experiencing anger. For instance, the parent can say to the child that if he is angry, it is fine, but, screaming, throwing things, hurting oneself, or physically hurting others are not going to be tolerated. To get in control of the emotion the child needs time alone to think about what has happened and to figure out what he or she needs.

We also teach our kids which things should be overlooked. For instance, if a child is angry because Mom said they would go to the movies, but something else came up and the movie got pushed to another date, I believe the child needs to accept the change and trust the parent that another day has been chosen for the theatre.

Anger can be dangerous to the person feeling it when it is impulsive and out of control. Such anger can act like a volcano, disrupting every good will and intention, tainting it with a desire for revenge. How can your children learn how to control anger? As a parent, we first model this for them. We teach them by displaying self-control when we communicate what we mean or how we feel when we get angry at them or at others. If you are having trouble displaying self-control and struggle with this, it is important to be honest and to admit your own challenges to your children, letting them know the actions you are taking in an effort to improve. You reinforce your children's healthy handling of their anger when they see you practise it in your own daily frustrations and irritations. You can also give your child examples of how you got angry at someone for whatever reasons and describe how you responded. Teach your children the difference between destructive and impulsive responses to anger and ones that are controlled and healthy. Usually children adopt their parent's method of dealing with anger.

When you teach your children healthy responses to anger you are taking the time to teach them good communication skills, and, in the process, giving them the tools they need to regulate themselves. You can ask a child to sit down, distract himself, go to the washroom, drink water and then talk it out if he would like to. It is important for the parent to just listen without interruptions. Be careful not to react to your children's anger by getting angry yourself or by shaming your children for being angry as this becomes an unhelpful double standard.

After a child has given his full explanation of his or her anger, the parent can help him or her by asking questions to further understand what is happening and see beyond the child's irritation. You are teaching him or her the importance of cooling off, stopping to think and filtering his or her thoughts, to know when it is appropriate to express feelings and to decide when things are better left unsaid.

The younger the child, the simpler a conversation can be and the more the parent needs to be involved at the moment the anger occurs. The older the child, the more accountability there should be. The parent may still need to be involved but the dynamic changes. The parent might not be there when the child becomes angry so it is crucial that the parent can share with the child a moment of feedback, asking the child to reflect.

Once one of my sons came home upset at his teacher about a sensitive topic that was being discussed at school. He had expressed his disagreement to the teacher over the matter. My son felt he was expected to tolerate views he disagreed with but also that the teacher was intolerant toward his beliefs. I supported his right to have an opinion and to voice his disagreement provided that he expresses it with respect and gentleness. It is important to try to understand others' beliefs even if understanding doesn't necessarily translate into acceptance of their beliefs. I told my son that he had a choice to excuse himself to get calm, talk to another available teacher or call me if the situation felt urgent.

As parents it is important to acknowledge our children's real struggles with disagreements. These moments are great opportunities to teach them how to handle those struggles on their own, to empower them to speak for themselves, and to support others who experience injustice or harm.

Teaching Values

Parents must teach their children values and morality even before they start school. Children need to learn from their parents the importance of respect, honesty, hard work, punctuality, and responsibility for one's words, attitudes, and actions. Children need to be grounded in these important aspects of life which will serve them well in their relationship with themselves and others.

A child who understands respect will treat others with the same dignity with which he or she wants to be treated, will ask the same for themselves, and will not tolerate abuse, victimization or any kind of manipulation or coercion. A respectful child will not be a bully in school and will know when to speak up against those who are behaving in a disrespectful way. A respectful child will not exploit younger children or those who are in any way vulnerable. A respectful child can be trusted.

Honesty is an essential quality to impart to your child. An honest child will have a hard time lying and will avoid it at most times. An honest child can be trusted. An honest child will not keep the truth from you even though telling it might be painful.

Training your child's character with honesty as a goal is hard work but achieves a result that your child and others in their life will be grateful for.

It is also important to me to impart a spirit of thankfulness in my children. Society needs grateful people rather than people who have a sense of entitlement and who believe others are there to serve them and make life easy for them. This is why, for instance, I would not give my child something they whined for at the supermarket. I prefer to give extras such as candy, toys or things one of my children wishes for when they are not expecting them. I might commend a child who has done a good act voluntarily or one who is taking the initiative to complete chores or a task. By doing this a child will learn to be grateful when getting things unexpectedly, instead of assuming they will get something "just because" they want it.

Regular practice in saying *please* and *thank you* and *may I please*, as well as asking permission to use other people's belongings is a must no matter how insignificant the favour is. Gratitude should not be conditional on the size or value of the favour or gift. I believe a child needs to learn that every time you or someone else does something they should say *thank you*, and not take it for granted or assume it was earned. "Thank you, Mom, for washing my clothes and putting them in their place" is an appropriate response.

Of course, as your child grows, you will be giving him or her more of their own things to take care of as well as additional chores around the house as an active participant and member of the family. To me, taking responsibility is another "must" among values I wish to impart to my child. This can start through the simplest of tasks such as putting back toys and picking up clothes. If your child can pick something up, then he or she is ready to learn how to put things back in their place. It will not be done perfectly or as quickly as a parent can do a task, but I encourage parents to wait for their child to finish picking up after themselves rather than trying do it all themselves. Avoid falling into the temptation of doing everything for your child. Remember the bigger they get, the more they should be able to do, and the less you, the parent should do.

Punctuality is important to teach although this becomes a sensitive topic if the parent is not punctual. If your children are of school age, they must learn to wake up by themselves, dress and wash themselves, and be ready for breakfast before leaving for school. They may need some help at the beginning but once you set this up as a daily routine, you will not be responsible for getting them ready and can enjoy your breakfast, prepare their lunches or use the time however you wish. I usually enjoy thirty minutes of quiet while I enjoy my breakfast; it is a time of reflection and getting mentally ready for what the day holds. I also use this time alone with God to meditate on Scriptures. I cherish this time because it is the fuel I need to continue and make sense of the day ahead.

Sadly, many parents rush around trying to get their kids ready or getting stuck in traffic trying to get late risers to school. They arrive at work tired, late, or both. I encourage you to decide what type of day you want and what type of child you are raising. It is not easy work, and we all make mistakes along the way, but it is important to remember to pursue the desired goals of responsibility, cooperation, and a character that will serve the child well throughout life.

Grandparents

Once while I was presenting a workshop on the Christian family, an elderly lady asked me what role grandparents should play in terms of rearing grandkids. Should they be involved in the rearing of grandkids? If so, to what extent? How much is too much involvement? What is not enough? These are interesting questions and can vary depending on culture.

In my Latin culture, the extended family plays a big role in the lives of children. I remember living with my single uncle and aunt and how they supported my parents in caring for me and my brother. I remember my uncle and aunt picking us from school, taking us to our extracurricular activities, taking us to birthday parties, helping us with homework, and always being around as we grew up. I have no regrets. As a child, I felt the world was a safe and friendly place especially with those two extra pairs of hands to look after us. The influence and time my uncle and aunt gave me greatly contributed in forming the person I am today.

I suggested to the woman who asked about the involvement of grandparents that the degree of involvement depends greatly on the parents of the children. For instance, if the grandparents have a strained relationship with the parents, this will be seen in how much time the parents allow grandparents in their kids' lives.

I once knew of a lady who crossed the limits. She was the stereotypical grandmother who loved to spoil her grandkids and did not have any regard for the rules the parents had set in place for their kids. This lady had no regards for her daughter-in-law's rules and limits. This grandmother reasoned, "I am the grandmother and I have the right to do as I pleased with my grandkids." That was, in my opinion, a big mistake. The daughter-in-law responded by setting limits in the relationship with this grandmother. In the end, it was a family loss: the kids lost out by not seeing more of their grandmother; the daughter-in-law lost out by not having a supportive relationship with her mother-in-law; and, the grandmother lost out by not being able to enjoy her grandkids.

My advice to grandparents is to listen to the parents and be involved as much as the parents allow. Take a supportive role and not a replacement role. Grandparents are not there to rear children in the place of parents, unless they have been appointed guardians or have been asked to take on a larger role.

Some grandparents may feel their children take advantage of them by burdening them with "time to be with your grandkids" as a weekly routine while the parents take a break from their own children. Grandparents should have the right to say "no" to their own kids in terms of babysitting or time spent with the grandkids. I tell parents that no one, not even their own parents, can ever fully substitute for them as parents.

Grandparents can offer support to the parents, as required and according to their abilities and openness, but adults are to be responsible for rearing and caring for their own children.

The involvement of grandparents in children's lives sends a message to the children that they are important and that many people love and care for them.

A non-involved parent or grandparent sends a very different message, one that says, "I have better things to do than spend time with you." It makes me think of a man I knew whose own father had worked three jobs when the man was a boy. They were new in the country and as foreigners the parents pursued the "American dream." One of the father's jobs was delivering pizza. One day, the boy had the bravery to call the pizza place, ask to speak to the store owner and once he was on the phone ask, "Please, fire my dad. I need to see him."

Grandparents can be a rare gift bestowed in our lives and the lives of our kids, so I encourage us to appreciate them.

Eating

Children will pick up their parents' habit of eating. I don't expect my child to eat what we don't eat or what is not being offered at home.

Sometimes parents ask me how I get my kids to eat vegetables. My answer is that whenever I prepare food, I set aside already cleaned and chopped vegetables. As my kids began to grow, I would offer them pieces of these vegetables and they would eat them as I prepared the food. Such a simple practice became a good habit in helping my kids eat a wide variety of nutritious food. You might notice that your child does not like a certain vegetable because it has a strong flavour but you may be able to entice the child to eat it with a pinch of lemon or salt.

Children need to trust their parents' knowledge of what is nutritious and healthy for growth. Parents don't need to explain nutrition facts or calorie intake to their young children who are not ready to receive that type of information. What parents need to do is to eat what they are expecting their children to eat. If all you eat is meat and potatoes, your children will likely not end up liking broccoli. Remember to not give children cookies, fruit, or candy on the side or as alternatives to more nutritious foods at mealtime. I remember a mother who told me that she brought chocolate to the table to remind her child that if he finished his meal, he would get chocolate as his treat. This mother could not understand why it became such a difficult challenge to convince her child to eat. She ended up giving the child a piece of chocolate with every spoonful of nutritious food that he ate. Every meal became a tiring ritual that was controlled by the child.

I want my children to learn to eat what I am offering them, considering that I know more about nutrition, calories, and balanced sources of energy. If parents don't know about good nutrition, I encourage them to learn what makes a healthy meal for a growing infant or child. As the parent, I'm responsible to provide what is best for my child's nutrition and growth.

For parents of picky eaters, eating times may be exasperating because meal time can take hours of cajoling, convincing or possibly threatening kids about eating. This might be followed by reheating the food if the child has not finished eating his or her meal in a normal time. Removing the food after fifteen to twenty-five minutes and setting it aside is a better idea. If one of my children won't eat what is being served, I don't feed them snacks or give alternatives. This allows the child to experience being hungry; when he or she is ready, I offer the meal as planned. It is amazing what hunger does to food preferences. A hungry person will usually eat whatever is being offered.

Once a child learns to eat food when offered, then the parent can provide, snacks and treats, but not before.

Sleeping

Children need to have a consistent time and their own bed or room for sleeping. Some exceptions might apply, during times such as sickness, sleepovers, camping, travelling or when visitors stay in the home.

Sleep time needs to be part of the schedule and routine that parents set. The appropriate time for children to go to bed will depend on their age. My children need approximately ten hours of sleep because they are early risers. By seven in the morning, they are usually up and running. Figuring out their bedtime is simple math, although I include another factor, which is my need for personal time and time with my spouse, as well as my own need for sleep. I put my kids to bed by seven-thirty p.m. If they don't want to sleep, I give them the option of reading quietly in their beds but by eight-thirty, lights will go out. While they are reading or talking quietly, I have the opportunity to spend time on the activities mentioned without interruptions, other than in case of emergencies. Fights between siblings who share a room are not emergencies but if they occur and I as a parent need to intervene, they will lose their hour of quiet time, and lights will go off immediately, even if it is summer and there is still daylight. (You might sense my frustration because this is an area of struggle for our family.)

As already mentioned, parents need private, uninterrupted intimate time. When my husband and I are feeling romantic, we would rather not be interrupted or questioned about why the bed might be creaking. Aside from instilling healthy sleep habits, establishing bedtime routines teaches children that parents need time together for entertainment, relaxation, and intimacy. Children need to learn to respect this time, for their own sake and for the sake of their parents' healthy relationship. Parents freely devote nurturing time to their children but claiming exclusive parental time is in no way neglectful.

Travelling

When travelling with children, our family's expectations are that they will sit and wait, talk, or calmly play among themselves, I usually provide them with useful tools. If we are travelling by air, I know that we will have several hours of waiting at the airport terminal. I usually take this time to get to know the airport and give my kids a tour. My purpose is to get them walking so that they will be tired by flight time. Before departure, I make sure they eat and use the restroom. By the time we board the plane, they are tired and usually ready to fall sleep. My airplane trips have been manageable and pleasurable without children crying, screaming, or asking constant questions. As kids get older, I encourage them to bring books, card games, electronic tablets, puzzles, and/or paper pads on which to write or draw. I explain the rules to them and give them options on how they can spend their time during our flight. I also pack a set of extra clothes in case of accidents and warm clothes for on-board climate changes.

Eating Out

Eating out can be an enjoyable activity or a dreary one. As a parent, I enjoy the opportunity of togetherness as a family. However, if children don't know how to behave themselves, some parents may avoid eating out or may do it regardless of a child's probable misbehaviour, thereby experiencing stress.

I recommend that parents take their children's misbehaviour seriously and correct it at every opportunity. If eating at home has become manageable then the next step is to eat out. Telling children the rules and expectations before going to the restaurant is important. Before we go to a restaurant, I may say, "We are going to the restaurant as a family. You will eat what we order for you, but you will have your choice of dessert once you are done with your meal. You will draw quietly and talk calmly. If your dad and I are speaking, I don't want interruptions unless you need to use the restroom."

These directions may change according to the child's age and the parents' level of comfort with the child's demonstrated behaviour outside the house. Some parents may give their children the choice of picking food for themselves. Depending on their maturity, children can participate meaningfully in conversations. Use what is best for your child and what works for you.

When misbehaviour happens in a restaurant, we remind our kids about the rules. We also have a routine where my husband will take a misbehaving child to the restroom for a talk while I wait. When they come back, all is usually settled and calm. We are spared embarrassment, and other restaurant patrons and servers are not made uncomfortable.

If misbehaviour persists after the restroom chat, my husband might take the child and their meals out to the car to wait while the rest of the family finishes eating. If misbehaviour continues, the next time the child will miss coming to the restaurant. If none of these approaches work, I tell my kids that they will be left behind with a babysitter, grandma or whoever volunteers to look after them while Dad and Mom go out to enjoy themselves. If they protest unfairness, we tell them that it is likewise unfair to go out and not have a peaceful time while eating because of unruly and embarrassing behaviour.

We have rarely gone to such extremes since all my kids typically have learned the lesson about how to behave in restaurants after they have been taken to the restroom. Every one of my kids has gone to the restroom once or twice with their father, with the lasting benefit being that we are now able to go out to eat without having a difficult time or a struggle with our children.

Shopping

Going shopping can be stressful. If every time you go shopping your kids throw temper tantrums because you won't buy them something they want, action must be taken. You can use the "restroom technique." If that doesn't work, I urge you not to make the mistake of promising to buy the child anything if he or she behaves. This would be training on how to be manipulative. I use distractions, such as saying, "Help Mommy with the shopping list. Every time I get an item, you put a check mark beside the item." I might ask my child what dessert or meal he thinks the family would like during the week. I could ask my child to help me write down the names of items while I'm making a shopping list at home. Also, if a child is old enough, you can ask him or her to get the shopping list items from the shelves and place them in the cart. At checkout, you can ask your child to pack items in the shopping bag. Show them how to bag groceries, especially if you have some items that are fragile and others that are heavy. It's worth mentioning that these shared activities can be fun for a parent as well as the child. It is rewarding watching your child help and take pleasure in helping.

Going shopping with your child can be a learning experience, too. As children get older, you can teach them about nutrition, calories, proteins, trans fats, sugars, etc., and how to compare less healthy food choices with better alternatives. You can also teach children basic math: adding the prices of the items in the cart; calculating how much the groceries will cost; looking for bargains and sales; and, thinking about a budget for future shopping. A child can learn to be a discriminating shopper, determining the relative value of goods and deciding which things might not be worth buying. Going shopping with your child can become a classroom of learning;

don't miss this excellent opportunity or get stuck in catering to your child's demands.

Chores

It is hard for some of us to get our children to participate in household chores. Between the whining, the comparisons with siblings who seem to have less work to do, the unfairness of life and the complaints of *I don't want to*, it's easy to understand how a parent might let their children off without participating in household chores.

As I said in the section on responsibility, when we ask our children to help us with chores, we are asking them to be an important and contributing part of the family. We are not only preparing them for the future by teaching them organizing and prioritizing skills, but we are giving them the satisfaction that comes from a job completed and well done.

Initially, if you are dealing with teens or children who are not used to helping and cooperating with chores around the house, expect a fight. A mother told me about her struggle with her teen daughter who took half a Saturday to clean the bathroom, a task that could be done in twenty minutes. This mom felt frustrated because of her daughter's slowness and lack of motivation to help in the cleaning. She asked me what she could do. I suggested that she first make her expectations clear, concise, and specific. For example, "I want you to clean the bathroom at ten a.m. and be done by eleven. I need the toilet, bathtub, mirror, vanity set clean. Please replace the dirty towels with new ones. Dirty clothes and towels go in the clothes basket in the basement. Thank you for helping." After the directions are given, the parent needs to go back and check when all is done. If the bathroom has been cleaned to the parent's satisfaction, she can compliment her daughter and express appreciation for her work.

If the chores are not done, then the child or teen needs to experience a consequence for not complying with the parent's stated expectations. The parent needs to pick consequences that are valued by the teen and that have some relationship to the task that has not been performed. The parent must be consistent in enforcing the consequence. Grounding your child for a month and giving in before the month is up is not a consequence. I suggest that parents relax, stay calm, and use creativity in imposing the consequence. We also need to remember that we are the authority.

I know of a father who told his teenaged daughter not to slam the door of her bedroom whenever she became upset. The daughter kept slamming the door without any regard for her dad's directive. In the end the father took the hinges off the door and removed the door from her bedroom, eliminating any sense of privacy she might want to have. It worked. When the door was replaced, the slamming stopped.

Another example involves a mother who kept asking her ten-year-old son to make his bed before leaving for school. The son would leave his bedroom untidy and his bed unmade despite his mom's insistence. One day, the mother became very creative and decided to take the bed away from her son's bedroom, to store it, and leave a sleeping bag in its place. She explained that he hadn't taken the time to make his bed and keep his bedroom tidy, so she had made the task simpler for him by reducing the contents of his bedroom. The mother made her point, and her child never again left an unmade bedroom.

These are just brief examples of solutions that parents can apply or adapt according to their situations and their children.

My sons have often come home from school with mud on their clothes, jackets, snowsuits and shoes. I would dutifully clean their clothes only to have my warnings about avoiding future messes ignored—I eventually concluded that my sons were actually rolling around in the mud. One day, the light went on. When one of my children next presented me with his muddy jacket to be cleaned, I asked him to accompany me to the laundry room where I showed him how to clean his own jacket. After a few minutes, I handed him the scrub brush and asked him to finish the job. As his eyes widened, I left him alone and went to make myself a cup of tea. I returned in a while to find him sweating and hard at work. And it worked! Any time I was faced with more muddy clothes, I would say, "You know where the laundry room is." I let go of the responsibility to care for my children's clothes when I decided they were fully capable of doing this themselves or at the very least making thoughtful choices.

Money

Should I pay my child for doing chores at home? This is a question I often hear parents ask. I believe that first we need to teach our children about the value of money and how to use it. I believe it is important to teach children how to spend, how to save, and how to give to others in need. A simple idea we use to teach our children about money divides it in thirds: spend one dollar; save one dollar; give one dollar to charity. It's an old rule that can be useful in today's world.

If my child wants to buy a book, a particular shirt, or some article with a higher price tag, I would encourage him to save for it. This, after all, is what adults must do if we are managing our finances sensibly. We allow our children to take responsibility for other-than-basic expenses by saving for them. We teach them that if they are receiving money, it is not to be used merely for their entertainment.

I believe that chores should be done without the expectation of payment because once you start paying your child for household chores, then you will end up giving raises and paying more than you initially expected. My recommendation is to pay your child when he or she unexpectedly performs something outside their area of responsibility. For instance, if your child decides to do some work in your garden, cleaning it up and planting some flowers, and does it to your satisfaction and delight, you can affirm him or her by giving money. But if your child performs tasks expecting payment, then he or she should not be "paid" with money. Children first need to learn to serve their families with an attitude of thankfulness and not with an expectation of getting paid.

Giving money to children, according to age-appropriateness and based on their level of responsibility, can help them understand its value and to appreciate the cost of things. Allow them to pay for full or part of their sports fees, books, lessons, and clothes as they get older. This will teach them money management and budgeting skills. It also shows them that by sharing in paying for their discretionary expenses, they are supporting the system that makes having money possible. As they grow up, children whose families use a system like this know when to spend, how much to save and how to attain their financial goals. These lessons are vital for avoiding disappointments and regrets in the future.

Pets

Having pets can be a wonderful opportunity to teach our children about responsibility, combining care with enjoyment. I suggest drawing up a contract between the parent and the child where the responsibilities of each are outlined clearly. (I have heard from too many parents who feel responsible for feeding, cleaning and looking after their children's pet.) The children might play an active role in drawing up the contract which each person then reads, approves, signs, and keeps a copy. Exceptions might be allowed when illness or vacation occur or when the child is clearly unable to meet the pet's needs and asks the parent to take over for a brief period of time. Ideally such a contract should be created before a pet is introduced into the home so that unforeseen failures might be avoided.

This pet's life depends on someone caring for it. Cleaning up after the pet is part of this responsibility. If a parent observes that their child has a difficult time keeping his or her bedroom tidy and organized, the parent needs to take this into consideration before the family takes on a pet. The principle I use that has served me tremendously is that if my children cannot be responsible for the minimum requirement of household responsibility, I would not want to add an extra responsibility that they would also fail to meet. If my children show responsibility in delivering on my expectations, I can expect that they will deliver on more demanding ones. For example, if my son has a small betta fish and he forgets to feed the fish and keep the bowl clean, I will likely not be convinced when he tries to persuade me that he will properly look after a dog. Once my son has learned to care for his fish, then he may be ready for a larger pet with more complex needs.

So, when do we introduce pets into the family? When our children are ready to care for them. By this, I do not mean that if I want a dog for my family that I should deprive myself of the opportunity since I am clear that this will be my responsibility and not my children's. I can ask my children to help me with the cleaning and feeding, but the responsibility rests on me. However, if my child asks for a pet, then we can apply the above suggestions with each parent making alterations that best suit his or her own family.

Homework

Doing homework with children can be a tedious and time-consuming job, especially for parents who hold full-time jobs outside and inside the home. I struggle in this area. Having five children between the ages of two to thirteen, I run a busy and noisy household. Plus, each one of my kids has different ways of learning, attention spans, and strengths and weakness in some areas of learning.

As children grow, parents need to be aware of all the information they get through media and other influences. The more we know of our children's world, the more tools we will have to guide them. In a way, children teach parents how to handle them. Parents need to be sensitive to each of their children's unique personalities and ways of understanding the world. Let us not commit the mistake of treating our children as robots, without personality or identity, who respond to stimuli and direction in the same ways.

As a parent, I need to be responsible for knowing each of my children and how I can best help them with their homework. I need to restrain the impulse to demand that they be excellent in an area, especially if they struggle in it. Sometimes learning takes longer than I anticipate. Children don't learn the same way. Some learn on their own, some by watching and imitating, some by listening, and others by constant repetition.

If you teach your children to be responsible and disciplined—that is, "This is *your* homework. I will help you with it but you are responsible for bringing it to me and asking for help"—and make sure they set aside daily uninterrupted time for homework, this will result in the development of healthy habits which will serve them well for the rest of their school years. Structure, consistency and repetition are key for the formation of habits.

Where your children do homework is important. If they are doing homework in the living room, make sure you are nearby, so you can periodically check on their progress and allow them to see you are available to help.

One of my sons is having difficulty with reading and writing. He is behind the reading level for his grade. I have spoken with the teacher and he is receiving extra help at school with reading buddies, at the library and with his own teacher. However, the teacher wants him to read to me or for us to read together every day. I admit that part of his delay is due to the fact that I have not been consistent in asking him to read to me. I have asked his elder siblings to help him out but because of temperament differences and arguing, my older kids have given up on helping him. This reminds me of the importance of making commitments as parents to paying attention to special needs of our children. It is all the more reason to look out for our own well-being, too, when dealing with unique challenges.

If you have a child like my eight-year-old who does not like to repeat the same tasks because he gets easily bored, frustrated and distracted, then you need to be creative in encouraging learning. My son would prefer to spend all his time on fun things such as sports. Here are some strategies I have used to encourage him: we split our child's homework times into intervals where he can read for five or ten minutes, then take a break for ten minutes, then come back to more reading, then break, and then finish his homework. In the break time, he can be allowed to go and play. We don't allow time for television or video games during this period since these take longer and can completely distract him from a studying frame of mind, with the result that the homework might not get finished. We explain all this ahead of time. He needs to uphold his end of the bargain about returning to work after the intervals or he will lose the privilege of this time-out.

For me, another challenge is finding the right environment where reading together will not be interrupted by an active two-year-old. I decided to put aside thirty minutes of time with my eight-year-old, explaining that I would play soccer with him for ten minutes and that afterwards we would spend the remaining twenty minutes reading or doing his homework. Part of my plan involves ensuring that my other children are busy in other ways so we don't get interrupted. So far we are having some success.

I understood that if I entered my son's world, namely sports, and interacted with him at his level, I would gain his attention when we sat down for homework. The challenge for parents is to find out what our child's interests are and to share in them. We can explain the trade-off: the child gets to participate in a favourite activity and have our undivided attention in exchange for applying him or herself to something that may be hard. Part of helping your child with homework is to learn how your child learns best. Pay attention to that and then try out some of your ideas with your child. If one attempt does not work, don't give up; try something else. Talk to teachers for ideas. Ask family members for suggestions. Once your children know how to do their own homework on their own, all you need to do is supervise or check that assignments are completed. Your children will be on their way to excel on their own.

The key in all this is setting aside the time to be with him or her and to help with whatever method of learning fits him or her. I don't say that my children need to try their best (they may have no idea what that is), but if I see that they are only making weak efforts, I do demand that they try to do better.

By no means does helping your child imply that you do their work. Instead, through getting to know how your child learns best, time on your part and steady practice, you will see results: your children succeeding in their learning, enjoying it, developing more curiosity, and engaging in their studies independently.

Hygiene

I have spoken with some parents who have adolescent children who do not take proper care of themselves. They will complain about their adolescent not brushing their teeth, not taking a shower, or not changing clothes regularly. Usually, this is accompanied by the teenager's apathetic or indifferent attitude to how he or she looks and smells. Cajoling the adolescent to be mindful about personal hygiene has limited success and slovenly behaviour becomes concerning.

It is important to observe any unwanted behaviour and to find out if there are any underlying causes. First, the parent must make sure there are no symptoms of mental or physical illness. I recommend the parent to take such a child to the family doctor for a consultation, talk to teachers to find out about school performance and the child's emotional demeanour at school. You may also wish to tactfully talk to their closest friends to inquire whether they have seen, heard or read anything unusual that may cause concern. Such an exploration regarding his child and his social network can be very revealing.

Any observation of changes in adolescents warrants attention, whether those changes are eating habits, time spent alone, misbehaviour, unusual drop-off in responsibility, sadness, irritability, an inability to connect with others, an inability to finish up homework, bullying and sexting, substance abuse, Internet pornography, abusive relationships, suicidal thoughts or attempts, etc.

Adolescence is a stage during which kids go through radical mental, physical and emotional changes. That is why is important for the parent to be able to detect the difference between what is normal change and what may fall outside the bounds of normal adolescent behaviour. Where there are concerns, a family doctor or counsellor can help a parent arrive at an understanding of what might be going on.

Returning to the subject of hygiene, a mother spoke with me, after ruling out any mental and physical illness, about her thirteen-year-old daughter's lack of proper hygiene. The mother complained that she had to wake the daughter up to make sure she showered before going to school. She was concerned that failing to have a daily shower would result in body odour and social issues.

In describing her situation, the mother told me about her recent marital separation because of chronic conflict with her husband over rearing and disciplining their three children. The mother admitted she was a permissive parent compared to her husband's severe authoritarian style.

I suggested the mother spend more time with her daughter, not only to remind her of her daily hygiene but to affirm her attractive appearance. I suggested the mother spend time on coaching her daughter on grooming, helping her daughter do her hair, introducing her daughter to basic cosmetics and generally emphasizing how looking good helps us feel good.

In the course of this training, the mother could pay close attention to the daughter's tastes and draw these out. I recommended that if the applied suggestions did not work after two weeks, the mother could consider allowing her daughter to experience feedback from her friends. This might be risky, however, because the peer treatment could involve rejection. In the end the mother did not need to go to such lengths. She came back to see me after a month and told me that spending more time with her daughter and guiding her in matters of physical appearance was producing results.

This story reminded me that sometimes our children want to communicate a feeling but do not know how to voice it. They may communicate it through an unpleasant behaviour. We must pay attention and try to find out what our children are trying to tell us. Often, if we give them more time, even if we find ourselves busy or distracted by other little ones, the undesired behaviour will go away. If it doesn't we need talk to the people with proper training to find out if there is more our child is dealing with. Never give up on finding out what is wrong or what went wrong. Assuming that the behaviour will pass is not always the right conclusion.

Quite possibly the most important gift our children need from us is the gift of time, freely given. This is not necessarily in the form of some activity but in being present for them, loving, playing, laughing, guiding, teaching, and empowering them on their journey toward becoming adults. What we value, they will value. As we practise our values, so will they. Even when we are not perfect, we can teach them that continued striving and living a responsible life in harmony with others is the path to success.

Conclusion

There is so much more I could say about how to help our children become responsible, caring and well-adjusted citizens, but in the end a great deal will depend on how much the parent gets to know their children and figures out how to raise them according to the inclinations the children bring into the world in terms of their strengths, abilities and talents. Let us be open in our parenting and receive every challenge as an opportunity for growth. We only have our children for such a short period of our lives and we want to learn how to best engrain in them how to become a person of good character who will pass on virtue to the next generation.

As parents, we have the responsibility to know who these people are, our children who are in our care for a short period of time and then are off to live their own lives and make their future families. As parents we have tremendous power to influence, to build on our children's innate gifts or to stifle them. How we relate, how we talk, how we treat them, and how we treat each other will inspire our children for the better or for the worse.

In the end, we want a final product that benefits the whole of society, where our communities become better because of the contributions of our kids; where families are strengthened because adults behave responsibly and are not diminished by egotistical and infantile grown-ups; where future generations are guaranteed a harmonious and civil society rather than a chaotic hedonistic society that serves only self-interested pleasure-seekers.

As parents we want to be able to transfer the best of ourselves in our children. Regrets are part of learning, so when we make mistakes, let us learn from them and let us not get paralyzed and stuck in our regrets. Every "I shouldn't have done that" is a teachable moment to do otherwise, to make adaptations. If you believe it is too late, because your kids are grown adults, think again. You may have grandkids; start making a difference with them.

If there are no children in your family, extend yourself to come alongside parents close to you, in your area, in your church, or anywhere there may be opportunities for you to offer words of wisdom, caution or encouragement, and to be a positive example. Look beyond yourself to see how you can reach other parents with your experience and knowledge. Turn any regrets you might have into opportunities for others to learn.

My hope is that this book has helped you look at parenting with fresh eyes, to become a more intentional parent, and to help others who could be struggling in their parenting to know that while it might seem at times to be an arduous task, it is an enormous privilege given to us to participate in the creation of good people. Think about it. We as parents are meaningful players in a grand design.

Acknowledgements

First, I would like to recognize the powerful and merciful role God has played in my life. Without Him I would have no purpose or goals to strive for. God has given me a thankful heart and has opened my mind to His wonderful creation. He has blessed me with a wonderful husband, who cares for me, tolerates my times away for studying, and is my anchor in times of self-doubts. God has been good to us and has multiplied our joy with our children.

Second, I thank my parents who have taught me by word and example how to live and go about living in this challenging world. They have given me the foundation of a life of faith, a life lived with love, hope, understanding and an openness to helping others.

I am grateful for my extended family and their role in providing support, excitement and the opportunity to learn and practise conflict resolution. My brother, Dr. Ricardo Martin Marroquín, in particular has given me valuable support, and encouragement to continue to share with others what I have acquired in my private readings and investigations. I am thankful for his love, patience and trust. Overall, my family has have offered. They have offered me insights on how to better communicate with others who are different.

I want to thank my dear friend Jeanette who has always taken the time to listen, support, and guide me in the midst of struggles. Through her observations on my relationship with my children, she provided the motivation that inspired me to share this material with others.

Laughter is a part of my life and I hope to keep bringing laughter into my kids' lives.

> *Train up a child in the way he should go [teaching him to seek God's wisdom and will for his abilities and talents], even when he is old he will not depart from it.*
>
> —Proverbs 22:6